THOROUGHBRED HORSES

by John Diedrich

CAPSTONE PRESS
a capstone imprint

Snap Books are published by Capstone Press,
1710 Roe Crest Drive, North Mankato, Minnesota 56003
www.mycapstone.com

Library of Congress Cataloging-in-Publication Data
Library of Congress Cataloging-in-Publication Data is available
on the Library of Congress website.
ISBN: 978-1-5435-0035-6 (hardcover)
ISBN: 978-1-5435-0041-7 (paperback)
ISBN: 978-1-5435-0047-9 (eBook PDF)

Editorial Credits
Amy Kortuem, editor
Kayla Rossow, designer
Morgan Walters, media researcher
Kathy McColley, production specialist

Image Credits
Getty Images: Bettmann, 9, Focus On Sport, 25, Hulton Archive, 6;
iStockphoto: WilliamSherman, 26; Newscom: John Dunn/Icon SMI, 19,
MARK ABRAHAM/UPI, 23; Shutterstock: Abramova Kseniya, Cover,
Angelique van Heertum, 11, blue67design, (floral sketch) design element
throughout, Dennis W Donohue, 20, Eduard Kyslynskyy, 5, Gary K Gray,
10, GeptaYs, 21, horsemen, 13, 16, 17, jacotakepics, 4, Juliata, (floral)
design element throughout, Kwadrat, 1, L. Kramer, (fish scale) design
throughout, Mikkel Bigandt, 14, Paul Aniszewski, 2, 3, redstone, (paper
background) design element throughout, suns07butterfly, (watercolor)
design element throughout, thomas carr, 29, yod67, (horse vector) design
element

Printed and bound in the USA.
010779S18

TABLE OF CONTENTS

CHAPTER 1

Born to Race

When people think of Thoroughbreds, they think of horse racing. Most racehorses are Thoroughbreds. Thoroughbreds **gallop** around racetracks at speeds up to 40 miles (64 kilometers) per hour.

The Thoroughbred is a young horse breed. The breed has existed for only 300 years. Some horse breeds began thousands of years ago.

In the 1500s horse racing was a popular sport in England. The fastest horses at that time were Arabians. English kings and other noblemen wanted to create an even faster horse breed.

gallop—a fast run

Thoroughbreds are famous for their speed.

THREE IMPORTANT STALLIONS

In 1688 Captain Robert Byerley captured a black Arabian **stallion** during a war in Hungary. After the war he took the stallion home to England. The horse was called the Byerley Turk.

The Darley Arabian was an important ancestor of today's Thoroughbreds.

stallion—an adult male horse that can be used for breeding

In 1704 Thomas Darley bought an Arabian stallion in Syria. He sent it to England. This horse became known as the Darley Arabian.

In 1724 an Arabian stallion was born in North Africa. The king of Tunis gave the young horse to King Louis XV of France. Englishman Edward Coke later bought the stallion. In 1729 Coke sold the horse to the Earl of Godolphin. People called the stallion the Godolphin Arabian.

These three Arabian stallions began the Thoroughbred breed. Their owners bred them to English racing **mares**. The stallions were sources of speed and spirit. The mares provided size and strength.

mare—an adult female horse

COMING TO AMERICA

In 1730 Bulle Rock became the first Thoroughbred stallion brought to the British colonies in North America. His father was the Darley Arabian, and his grandfather was the Byerley Turk.

In 1805 the stallion Sir Archy was born in Virginia. He became the top racehorse in the United States. Later Sir Archy's owners used him to establish the Thoroughbred breed in the United States. He also was an important **ancestor** of the American Quarter Horse breed.

MOVING WEST

Most early U.S. Thoroughbred breeders lived in Virginia. In the 1800s settlers began to move west. They took their Thoroughbreds with them. Tennessee and Kentucky became top horse-producing states. Thoroughbreds still graze on the bluegrass pastures of Kentucky.

By the 1820s Kentucky had many racetracks. The town of Lexington became famous for horse breeding and racing.

ancestor—a member of a breed that lived a long time ago

Man o'War

Many racing experts believe Man o'War was the greatest racehorse ever. This chestnut horse was born in 1917. He had a stride that was 28 feet (8.5 meters) long.

In two years of racing, Man o'War won 20 of his 21 races. After he retired, Man o'War sired many top racers. His son War Admiral won the Triple Crown in 1937.

When Man o'War died in 1947, his owners placed his body in a large coffin. Racing fans from around the world came to say good-bye to the great horse. People still visit his grave at the Kentucky Horse Park in Lexington.

Even as foals, Thoroughbreds are athletic and spirited.

AMERICAN JOCKEY CLUB

In 1894 a group of Thoroughbred owners formed the American Jockey Club in New York City. Owners register their Thoroughbreds' names and ancestry with this organization.

Today the American Jockey Club accepts about 22,500 new **foal** registrations each year. This number makes the Thoroughbred one of the most popular breeds in the United States. The Jockey Club also registers Thoroughbreds born in Canada and Puerto Rico.

FACT

In 1938 Seabiscuit was a small Thoroughbred with crooked knees. Yet he managed to beat the top racehorses of the day. Seabiscuit's story was made into a popular movie in 2003.

foal—a horse that is less than 1 year old

Chapter 2
Speed and Style

The Thoroughbred is a tall breed. Horses are measured in hands. One hand equals 4 inches (10 centimeters). An average Thoroughbred's height is 16 hands at the **withers**.

BUILT FOR SPEED

The Thoroughbred's body is well suited for racing. The Thoroughbred's long, sloped shoulders and powerful **hindquarters** give it a longer stride than horses of other breeds. Thoroughbreds also have long, powerful muscles that allow them to explode with speed.

withers–the top of a horse's shoulders

hindquarter–the part of a horse where the back leg and rump connect to the body

The Thoroughbred has a longer stride than many other breeds do.

Some tall horses are heavy, but the Thoroughbred is sleek and slender. The Thoroughbred's slender body helps it run fast.

Chestnut is a common Thoroughbred coat color.

A Handsome Breed

The Thoroughbred's appearance is a reminder that its ancestors were Arabians. Arabian horses are known for their beauty. Thoroughbreds have wide foreheads and large, dark eyes. Thoroughbreds also have thinner, longer necks than most breeds.

Thoroughbreds can be many colors. Brown, bay, and chestnut are common colors. Bay horses are red-brown with black lower legs and black manes and tails. Chestnut is a shade of copper or red.

Thoroughbreds can also be black, gray, white, palomino, or roan. Palomino horses are tan with lighter manes and tails. Roan horses have coats of a solid color mixed with white hairs.

Personality

Thoroughbreds' personalities also make them good racehorses. Thoroughbreds are intelligent and spirited. They seem to enjoy the competition of racing. Off the track, most Thoroughbreds are gentle and cooperative. They tend to form strong bonds with their trainers or handlers.

powerful hindquarters

long, slender legs

withers

wide forehead

long, slender neck

sloped shoulders

deep chest

CHAPTER 3

Training for the Track

Thoroughbred racehorses begin their training shortly after birth. The horses are broke for riding late in their first year. Thoroughbreds are ready to race at 2 years old.

RACE TRAINING

Experienced riders called trainers work with Thoroughbred racehorses. The trainers decide how the horses will be worked each day.

The trainer works with an exercise rider. The trainer tells the exercise rider how far and how fast to ride the Thoroughbred.

Exercise riders help keep racehorses in top condition.

Some days the horse is ponied around the track. While riding another horse the exercise rider leads the Thoroughbred around the track. The exercise rider also takes the horse for long jogs and slow gallops around the track. These exercises get the Thoroughbred in racing shape.

Young Thoroughbreds in good condition can gallop at a high speed, or breeze. When the Thoroughbred is breezing the trainer times it with a stopwatch. The trainer times the horse to make sure it is getting faster. If it is not, the trainer changes the horse's training.

FACT

All Thoroughbreds have an official birthday of January 1. A horse born December 31 would be considered 1 year old the next day. This rule makes it easier to keep track of horses' ages for racing purposes.

RACING

Thoroughbreds may enter their first races as 2-year-olds. These races are called baby races. Thoroughbreds usually run in only a few baby races. Young horses that are raced too much can become injured.

At 3 years old, Thoroughbreds can enter more races. Some owners retire their horses after the second year of racing. Others race their horses as long as they continue to win. Some Thoroughbreds still race at age 10 or older.

Chapter 4

Thoroughbreds in Action

Thoroughbreds race on dirt or grass tracks. Races are measured in furlongs. Each furlong is one-eighth of a mile (.2 kilometer). Races are usually 4 to 9 furlongs in length.

The most famous Thoroughbred race is held each year at Churchill Downs in Louisville, Kentucky. The first Saturday in May, the world's fastest 3-year-old Thoroughbreds race in the Kentucky Derby.

The Kentucky Derby is the first of three races called the Triple Crown. The second race is the Preakness Stakes in Baltimore, Maryland. The last race is the Belmont Stakes. The Belmont is run at Belmont Park in New York.

In 2017 Always Dreaming
won the Kentucky Derby.

Triple Crown winners are rare. Since 1875 only 12 horses have won the Triple Crown. The last horses to win the Triple Crown were Secretariat in 1973, Seattle Slew in 1977, Affirmed in 1978, and American Pharoah in 2015. Since then, several horses have won the Derby and the Preakness but have lost the Belmont.

The Triple Crown races are the most famous horse races. But there are many other races. Some Thoroughbreds travel around the world during their racing careers.

Eye on the Prize

Racehorses compete for prize money called a purse. Each race has a purse that is split among owners of the top horses. Some races have purses of millions of dollars.

In North America, the largest purse is at the Breeders' Cup World Thoroughbred Championships. The top racehorses compete at this event in early November. Its races offer purses of more than $25 million.

Secretariat

In 1973 a large chestnut Thoroughbred won the Triple Crown. His name was Secretariat.

Secretariat was born in 1970 in Virginia. By age 2, he stood 16.2 hands and weighed 1,200 pounds (544 kilograms).

The big red horse had an amazing racing career. Secretariat set track records with his winning times at the Kentucky Derby and the Preakness. At the Belmont, he finished the race 31 lengths ahead of the second-place finisher. His time of 2 minutes, 24 seconds set a world record.

Secretariat sired championship foals before he died in 1989. In 2004 his great-great-grandson Smarty Jones won both the Kentucky Derby and the Preakness Stakes.

OTHER COMPETITIONS

Not all Thoroughbreds are racehorses. Thoroughbreds also do well at jumping, fox hunting, and **dressage**. In dressage competitions, horses perform a series of advanced movements.

Some riders use Thoroughbreds in fox hunting events.

Thoroughbreds also compete in horse shows. Thoroughbreds do well in English riding classes and in timed events.

THOROUGHBRED CARE

Like all horses, Thoroughbreds need a great deal of care. Top racehorses live in air-conditioned stables with trainers and veterinarians on call. Horses used for jumping, dressage, or shows may not live in such grand surroundings. But they still need a barn or stable for shelter and a large pasture where they can graze and run.

The thrill of the Triple Crown excites racing fans each spring. At the center of it all are the Thoroughbreds. These strong, graceful athletes are born to run.

FACT
Only three winners of the Kentucky Derby have been fillies. These young female horses were Regret in 1915, Genuine Risk in 1980, and Winning Colors in 1988.

dressage—a riding style in which horses complete a pattern while doing advanced moves

Fast Facts:
The Thoroughbred Horse

History: The Thoroughbred breed began about 300 years ago when people brought Arabian stallions to England and bred them to the local mares. The first Thoroughbred came to North America in 1730.

Height: 15 to 17 hands (about 5 feet or 1.5 meters) tall at the withers. Each hand equals 4 inches (10 centimeters).

Weight: 900 to 1,200 pounds (408 to 544 kilograms)

Colors: bay, brown, chestnut, black, gray, white, palomino, roan

Features: tall, lean body; slender, well-muscled neck; long, slender legs; deep chest; wide forehead; large eyes

Personality: intelligent, spirited

Abilities: Thoroughbreds are best known for racing. They are also used for shows, jumping, fox hunting, and dressage.

Life span: 20 to 30 years

Glossary

ancestor (AN-sess-tur)–a member of a breed that lived a long time ago

dressage (druh-SAHJ)–a riding style in which horses complete a pattern while doing advanced moves

foal (FOHL)–a horse that is less than 1 year old

gallop (GAL-uhp)–a fast run

hindquarter (HIND-kwor-tur)–the part of a horse where the back leg and rump connect to the body

mare (MAIR)–an adult female horse

register (REJ-uh-stur)–to enter a horse's name and ancestry with an official club

stallion (STAL-yuhn)–an adult male horse that can be used for breeding

withers (WITH-urs)–the top of a horse's shoulders

Read More

Buckley, James Jr. *Who Was Seabiscuit?*
Who Was ...? New York: Grosset & Dunlap, 2015.

Fishman, Jon M. *American Pharoah.* Amazing
Athletes. Minneapolis: Lerner Publishing Group, 2016.

Kolpin, Molly. *Favorite Horses: Breeds Girls Love.*
Crazy About Horses. Mankato, Minn.: Capstone
Press, 2015.

Internet Sites

Use FactHound to find Internet sites related to this book.

Visit *www.facthound.com*

Just type in 9781543500356 and go.

 Check out projects, games and lots more at
www.capstonekids.com

InDex